BY BRITTNI DE LA MORA

—

14 WAYS TO
KEEP YOUR
LOVE ON FIRE
FOR HIM

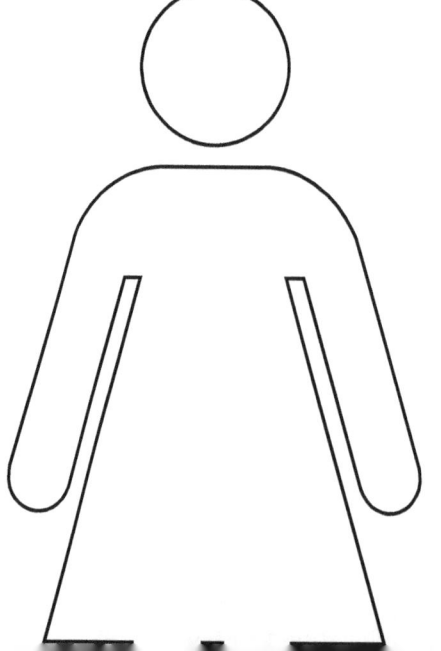

Copyright © 2018 Fireproof Ministries

All rights reserved. No portion of this book may be reproduced, stored in a retrieval system, or transmitted in any form or by any means—electronic, mechanical, photocopy, recording, scanning, or other—except for brief quotations in critical reviews or articles, without the prior written permission of the publisher. Published in Pasadena, CA by Fireproof Ministries. Fireproof Ministries titles may be purchased in bulk for educational, business, fundraising, or sales promotional use. For information, please e-mail **info@fireproofministries.com**.

Unless otherwise noted, Scriptures are taken from the New International Version®, NIV®, The Message, New Living Translation, New King James Version, and The English Standard Version, New American Standard Bible, King James Version. Copyright © 1973, 1978, 1984, 2011 by Biblica, Inc.™ Used by permission from Zondervan. All rights reserved worldwide.

www.zondervan.com.

The Library of Congress Cataloging-in-Publication

Data is on file with the Library of Congress

ISBN-13: 978-0692078952

Contents

CHAPTER ONE
Dream on Purpose   08

CHAPTER TWO
Break the Routine   13

CHAPTER THREE
Declare It   18

CHAPTER FOUR
Intentional Devotionals   23

CHAPTER FIVE
Build the Bridge to Communication   28

CHAPTER SIX
To Serve Not to Be Served   34

CHAPTER SEVEN
Pause for Celebration   39

CHAPTER EIGHT
Disconnect from What's Disconnecting You   44

CHAPTER NINE
Consumed by Comparison   49

CHAPTER TEN
Love Keeps Record of Rights   54

CHAPTER ELEVEN
The Little Things Matter   58

CHAPTER TWELVE
Wisdom Seekers   63

CHAPTER THIRTEEN
The Beauty in the Struggle   68

CHAPTER FOURTEEN
L.O.L Love Out Loud   73

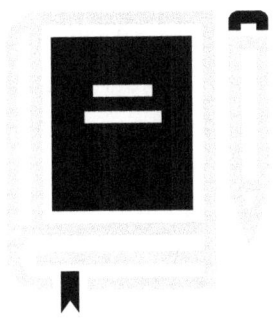

How to get the most out of this book

Don't you just love the feeling of buying something new? For instance, when you get a new car, a new pair of shoes, or a new outfit? There's nothing like the excitement that comes from getting something new. We designed this book to create that kind of feeling in you and your significant other. There is an old saying that when you get into a relationship, the excitement stops there, but we believe when you get into a relationship it only gets better.

This book will reignite the fire and passion in your relationship. What you are saying by taking on this 14-day challenge with us is that keeping the flame of love burning within your relationship matters. You don't get a fire simply because you want one, you get a fire because you create one. This challenge will create that fire. This book was designed to ensure that not only will the fire in your relationship with your partner grow, but the fire in your relationship with God will grow as well.

We have written this book for those who are dating, engaged and even for those whom are married. This book is meant to be a 14-day challenge; however, we understand that if you are dating you may not see each other daily. So, feel free to take as long as you need with this book. Something you may notice about the two different books is the chapter titles and challenges are the same. The challenges are the same, because we want you to do them together. However, the content is different because Britt wrote from her perspective to the women and I wrote from my perspective to the men. In the future, if the two of you want to take this 14-day challenge again, we encourage you to do so. You could even switch books to get a completely different perspective. We believe God will speak to you differently every time you read this book because as time passes and new experiences come your way, your outlook will change. We encourage you take this challenge once a year to keep the fire in your relationship or marriage burning. We are so excited for what God is going to do in your lives and we pray that your relationship will always remain fresh and on fire.

This book follows along with the 14 videos created by Rich and Britt. Please send an email to **14days@strongermarriages.com** and we will send you a link to access the video series. If you have any issue reach out to us at **info@strongermarriages.com**.

*Thanks,
Rich and Britt*

CHAPTER ONE

—

Dream on Purpose

My husband and I continuously dream on purpose. At the end of every year, we celebrate what we have conquered, and we plan our next moves by writing out our goals. Throughout each year we remind each other of what we are fighting for within those goals. When you have a dream or a vision together, it can make even the most difficult seasons of life seem so purposeful. Nothing seems like an accident when you have a dream.

Dreaming together as a couple creates a purposeful couple. When you dream together, you no longer make moves just because you have to; you begin to make moves that are directly aligned with your dream. You begin to understand that to fulfill a dream you must take purposeful steps to get there.

I have learned that your steps will either determine your outcome or your desired outcome will determine your steps. If you don't know what your outcome is, because you haven't dreamt on purpose yet, then your steps can become meaningless because they aren't being led by your dreams.

Martin Luther King Jr. changed the course of history because he had a dream. He began to take bold steps that were in alignment with his dream in hopes that his dream would become a reality. Because his steps had a purpose, his dream became a reality.

Imagine the great change that would happen in our relationships if we all began to dream on purpose. There is nothing like a couple who is walking with purpose. A couple walking with purpose is unstoppable because they know what they are fighting for and they will not stop until they arrive with a victory.

Proverbs 29:18 (KJV) says, *"Where there is no vision, the people perish."*

Have you ever encountered a couple that is moving but they are not going anywhere? Could it be that the reason why they aren't going anywhere is that they don't have a vision for their relationship? Without a vision or a plan, a relationship cannot healthily stand. It is important that you communicate with your partner to decide what the two of you want to conquer together. Your relationship is meant to be purposeful, but if you don't have a vision together then what you are saying is, "We have no future together."

I am often most inspired by Joseph in the Bible. Genesis 37:9 teaches us that Joseph dreamt again. I believe this is what we need to do in our relationships. We need to dream again. We need to pray for our God-given destiny and potential so that we have something to look forward to, and something to hope for so that we can work together as a team to conquer our dreams. I believe that as you dare to dream on purpose with your partner and work together to make your dream become a reality, not only will your relationship stay fresh & exciting, but you will become a couple who inspires others to become visionaries. If the Scripture teaches us that where there is no vision the people perish, then this means that where there is a vision, the people will be revived.

Today, it is time to revive the fire in your relationship. My husband and I challenge you to dream on purpose with your partner. Pray and take as much time as you need to create a vision for your future. Write down your goals on the pages we have provided along with a plan of attack. What does the future of your relationship look like and what steps will you take to get there?

Journal below:

Write what you learned today, how it went and what memories were made.

CHAPTER TWO
—
Break the Routine

I am the type of woman who loves a routine, especially when it comes to health and fitness. You'll find me at the gym at the same time every day, you will find me watching various health food documentaries on Netflix, and you will regularly find me eating the same types of meals repetitively for breakfast, lunch, and dinner. It's just the way I am. I have become wired to my fit routine because my health is important to me. I have found what works, so I stick with it. My husband, on the other hand, is still getting used to my healthy lifestyle. He knows it's important not only for me to eat healthy, but for him as well, yet he isn't quite excited about eating the same dinner night after night. The other day he came along to the grocery store with me, and I felt horrible when he asked, *"Do we have to have salad AGAIN?"* I thought, *"Wow, I am boring my husband with the types of food that I love."*

This conversation opened my eyes. I realized that to keep my husband satisfied in our marriage and keep him from growing bored (which in this case he already had), I have to break the routine. Repetitive dinners are an easy fix. The real caution lies in a routine love life. It's imperative we learn to switch things up. The last thing we as women want in our relationships is to become completely predictable to our men. Men love thrill and excitement. I mean, have you ever watched your man watch his favorite sports game? I believe the reason they love sports so much is that sports are unpredictable and thrilling.

Ladies, do you know who else was completely unpredictable? Jesus! Yes, Jesus. One moment He tells a man with a skin disease to *"Be healed,"* and then in another moment He spits in the dirt, makes mud with it and puts it on the eyes of a blind man so that he could be healed. Jesus could have commanded the blind man to be healed just as He did to the man with the skin disease, but He didn't. Jesus was a man who kept people guessing what He was going to do next. Let's break the routine in our love life and keep our men guessing what we will do next.

I bet you're asking yourself, *"What does that look like for me?"* Switch things up. Well, what is something your partner would love for you to do that maybe you haven't wanted to do in the past? Could it be enjoying his favorite sports game with him or listening to the music he likes? Instead of going out to eat, you could cook him his favorite meal or vice versa. If you're married, I would suggest you get dolled up for your husband and show him just how much you love him (wink wink). My point is, do something out of the ordinary. You know your partner better than I do. Think about what he likes and go for it!

Today, it is time to revive the fire in your relationship. My husband and I challenge you and your partner to break the routine. Use some of the examples that I have provided in the paragraph above, or come up with something exciting, creative, and heartfelt on your own. Do something unexpected. Your husband, or husband-to-be, will appreciate the surprise romantic gesture more than you know. Journal about your experience below and remember that breaking the routine should become a part of your routine.

Journal below:

Write what you learned today, how it went and what memories were made.

CHAPTER THREE

—

Declare It

Between the ages of 16-22, I got eight tattoos marked on my body. One day I woke up and thought, *"What have I done? I don't want tattoos anymore."* From this day forward I would respond to any compliments and comments about my tattoos by saying, *"Thank you, but I am getting them removed."* They would ask questions like, *"Why are you getting them removed?"* and *"Who is removing them?"* I always had an answer to their first question, I knew why I wanted them removed, but I had no idea who was going to remove them. I just knew, that somehow, someway, someday, God would provide. So, I continued to speak it out to all who asked. To get them removed, it was one of those cases when I desperately needed God's provision because I was working a near to minimum wage job. I found out that my tattoos were going to cost about $40,000 to remove. I did not have that kind of cash floating around. However, 2 Corinthians 5:7 (NKJV) teaches that we walk by faith and not by sight; and Proverbs 18:21 (NASB) teaches us that death and life are in the power of the tongue. I refused to allow my *"sight"* to dictate my faith, and I certainly was not going to allow my tongue to speak death over my blessing. I refused to allow my circumstances to bring me down. By sight, I was living paycheck to paycheck, and there was no way I could afford the luxury of tattoo removal. But by faith, I serve a God who can do immeasurably more than all I could ask for or imagine. So, I chose to walk by faith, and I am glad I did.

One night, I got a call from a friend of mine, who had complimented my tattoos two years prior. My response had stayed in the back of her mind. She called me that evening because she was at a ministry meeting and overheard a woman talking about her non-profit organization that *"Removes the reminders of your past."* This woman started an organization to remove tattoos for free and was looking for people who might be interested in her services. With my words, I sowed a seed of faith, and two years later reaped the harvest of the blessing I desired. I have been getting my tattoos removed free for the past few of years. God's generosity has saved me at least $40,000 in treatment.

Question: What words are you declaring over the future of your relationship? If you have the power to create and destroy simply with the words you speak, then are you creating or destroying your future? When the apostles were out preaching the good news, they weren't forbidden to perform miracles; they weren't forbidden to heal, they were forbidden to speak in Jesus's name. Why? Because when you speak in His name, miracles begin to happen. When you speak in His name, lives begin to change. When you speak in His name, you create blessings for your future. Again, I ask what words are you speaking? I can tell you what your future looks like based on the words you are declaring in the present. If you want a marriage that lasts a lifetime, declare it. If you want financial freedom, declare it. If you want children who desire to seek the Lord, declare it. Your future is in your mouth.

Today, my husband and I challenge you to fast all negative talk for the remainder of this book. When you take out the negative talk, it means you will not allow words to be spoken from your mouth that are not in alignment with the word of God. We want you both to select a Scripture you can declare over your circumstances. We believe that as you do this, your circumstances will come into alignment with the word of God. Journal the circumstances you want to see a change in and write down the Scripture you will declare over them. Rich and I pray God's favor and blessing over your lives. Have fun with this challenge!

Journal below:

Write what you learned today, how it went and what memories were made.

CHAPTER FOUR
—
Intentional Devotionals

I am a firm believer in there being nothing more important than spending time with God every morning. When I fail to spend time with God in the morning, it throws my entire day off. Without God, I lack peace, patience, wisdom, love, joy; the list goes on and on. Before getting married, spending time with God was easy. I woke up alone and had no one to look after other than myself. I would wake up, make my cup of tea and then get right into my devotion time. The morning I woke up next to my husband was the day I realized things had changed. I had to become extremely intentional about spending time with God because if I didn't, then the distraction of my new morning routine would distract me from spending time with God. Ladies, I don't know about you, but I need Jesus. Without Him, I can be a little cranky, but with Him, I am full of grace. If you're married, then you know that grace will take your marriage to heights that impatience could never reach.

When you spend time with God, His attributes become your attributes; and His attributes will always better you and your relationship. Marriage is a partnership, and when you don't spend time with God, you end up placing the burden on your husband. When the storms of life hit, we need God's direction, and when making life decisions, we need God's counsel. But, if we aren't seeking Him, how will we recognize His voice when He is speaking?

For my husband and I, God has always taken first place in our relationship and now in our marriage. When we were dating, we would each seek God first, and then we would schedule a phone call before work to talk about how God spoke to us that morning. This unfading trend has transferred into marriage with us. We now seek God one-on-one followed by a discussion over breakfast. We understand our marriage is destined to succeed when God is the foundation we build on.

"Though one may be overpowered, two can defend themselves. A cord of three strands is not quickly broken." – Ecclesiastes 4:12 (NIV)

I love this Scripture because it is a reminder that when you and your partner stand firm in God, you form a three-strand cord that cannot be quickly broken. Remember John 10:10 (NIV) says, *"The thief is out to steal, kill, and destroy,"* so we need to be intentional with our devotionals, so the enemy can't destroy the union God has brought together. When you keep God at the center of your relationship, He will become the foundation on which you build on. If you build on anything other than God it is as though you are building on the sand. The unfortunate thing about this is that when the storms of life hit they are bound to destroy all that was built on sand, because sand is not a firm foundation. If we want marriages that last a lifetime, we must build on God who is the rock that will sustain us through the worst of times and the best of times.

Today, my husband and I challenge you to be intentional with your morning devotionals. We challenge you to seek God before you seek each other. After seeking God, we encourage you to talk about how God spoke to each of you in your time of study and prayer. Remember, as you first seek God not only will all your needs be provided for, but your love for Him will grow as well. As your love for God grows, so will your love for each other. Make sure to journal about your experience and have a blessed time with God.

Journal below:

Write what you learned today, how it went and what memories were made.

CHAPTER FIVE

Build the Bridge to Communication

Let's face it, men and women communicate differently. Some would even say, we speak different languages. Never have I found this statement to be truer until marriage. When my husband communicates, he gives me the bare minimum, which to him is all I need to know. He communicates with the *"give her the meat, throw away the bone"* mentality. However, I want the meat, the bone, the fat, the seasoning, the marinade, the cooking temperature, and the cook time type of conversations. Ladies, are you with me?

My style of communication works well when I'm out with the girls, but could cause my husband to get lost in translation. Most men just can't keep up with our style of communication. I once heard a preacher say, *"Men speak in straight lines, but women speak in circles. Women are like airplanes circling the runway before they land the plane."* I laughed when I heard this because it's just the way God wired us. As women, we are detail oriented. Many of us like to color coordinate our outfits with the perfect number of accessories; others are brilliant artists never missing a detailed stroke with the paintbrush and others can get down in the kitchen without a recipe using not one drop too much of that homemade marinade. In some areas of your life, you are a detailed woman because God made you that way and you should be proud.

I have learned that if we want to be effective communicators, we need to communicate on the level our partners best receive it. For example, my husband is a goal-oriented, straight-to-the-point kind of man. He is also the primary breadwinner in our household. So, when I go to the grocery store, I often ask him, *"Love, can you send me some money please?"* He responds with, *"How much?"* I used to respond with, *"Well, we need almond milk, veggies, oatmeal, water…"* But then he would cut me off with, *"Love, I did not ask what we need, I asked how much do you need?"* I've learned that a simple conversation can quickly become a frustrating one if I don't communicate with my husband's level of communication. We had to learn to build the bridge to communication because a bridge that is never built is a bridge that can never be crossed. Learning to communicate on a person's ability to receive what you are communicating will not only help you in your marriage, but also in your career, in ministry, and in every type of relationship you encounter.

Ineffective communication leaves room for assumptions, arguments, and confusion. Do you remember in Genesis 11 when God confused the language of the people because they were building a tower that was so high it would make their names famous as opposed to His? When they spoke the same language and were unified, they were building something so great that it got the attention of heaven. I understand that we are called to make God's name great and not our own (which is why He confused their language). However, this Scripture teaches us that when we speak the same language and are unified, we can build something so great it will catch the attention of heaven. To build something great with our partner, we must speak the same language. May your language be concise, edifying, challenging, and inspiring one another to build your God-given dream.

Now that we understand effective communication, we must understand that disagreements will happen in every relationship. Keeping your relationship fresh and exciting is important in building an effective bridge to communication in times of dispute as well. There are two Scriptures I meditate on to remind myself of how I should react in times of dispute. The first Scripture is Matthew 5:9 (NIV). It says, *"Blessed are the peacemakers, for they will be called children of God."* When you converse with your partner, can God call you His child? Do you bring peace or chaos into your relationship with the words you speak? Because this Scripture teaches us that God calls the peacemakers His children, we need to learn to bring peace into our household. We are lead right into the second Scripture, Galatians 5:22-23 (NLT), *"But the Holy Spirit produces this kind of fruit in our lives: love, joy, peace, patience, kindness, goodness, faithfulness, gentleness, and self-control."* Your words should produce this kind of fruit. A dispute is not the time to get loud, it's not the time to bash your partner with unkind words, nor is it the time to shut down and stay silent. A dispute is a time to build the bridge to communication by staying calm so that you can safely cross the bridge built with words that bare the fruit of the spirit. This type of bridge will lead to a solution to any problem that may occur in your relationship or marriage.

Today, my husband and I challenge you to have a conversation with your partner about how you can effectively build the bridge to communication. Discuss how the different Scriptures we have given you speak to you, and how you will apply them to your everyday life. Rich has provided a different Scripture for your man, but go ahead and write all of them down. Next, we would like for both of you to post them on the refrigerator, or on your desk so you can continue to meditate on them. The next time one of you is not understanding one another, or a disagreement arises, remember what you have learned today and apply these Scriptures so you can build an effective bridge to communication that will lead you both to a solution. Journal about how this conversation has helped you grow today and refer back to it when necessary.

Journal below:

Write what you learned today, how it went and what memories were made.

CHAPTER SIX
—
To Serve Not to Be Served

"Whoever wants to be a leader among you must be your servant, and whoever wants to be first among you must be your slave. For even the Son of Man came not to be served but to serve others and to give his life as ransom for many."
Matthew 20:27-28 (NLT)

This Scripture teaches us that the measure of greatness is not position, power, or prestige, it's service. If you want to be great amongst others, it comes from serving them. Think about it this way; you have two friends; one is spoiled, and the other is a servant. The one who is spoiled always takes from you, giving nothing in return. You're both freezing, but she would take the shirt off your back. Your other friend will stop at nothing to see you get ahead in life. She doesn't care to take much from you but always wants to give to you. She sows into your dreams and loves you for who you are, not for what you can give. Answer honestly, which friend is going to hold a greater position in your heart? My guess is, you answered the servant. Why? Serving elevates us.

There is no greater way to enter new levels in life than to serve. Serving others will unlock doors of opportunity and will bring forth unimaginable blessings into your life. Since the day I met Jesus, I have pretty much lived at church. I love being in God's presence, and I love serving others. Serving others is what caught the attention of my husband. My husband was looking for a woman who loved to serve others because it showed him that she was selfless. You can't be selfish and serve others at the same time. Selfish people don't have time to think about anyone other than themselves.

I love the book of Ruth in the Bible. Naomi and Ruth entered a major season of heartbreak. Naomi lost her husband and her two sons, and Ruth lost her husband. Through this time all they had was each other. Even though Ruth had to manage her heartbreak and loss, she never stopped serving her mother-in-law, Naomi. Through serving, God unlocked His supernatural favor upon Ruth by blessing her with a wealthy God-fearing husband. I wonder what her life would have been like if she was consumed with herself with no desire to serve. Would God have blessed her the same? I don't believe so. It was her service that caught the attention of her new husband, Boaz.

If you want to unlock God's supernatural favor in your life, then start serving! When you serve people, you'll catch the attention of heaven and God will promote you. Today, my husband and I challenge you and your partner to have an honest discussion about serving. Do you currently serve? Do you serve in a church, in your community, and in your household? If so, how have you seen God move in your life through your acts of service? If you don't currently serve, we challenge you both to serve together in your local church or community. When you give back to God's people, He will give back to you. Serving others will grow you as a couple as you plant yourself in God's house. Through serving, you will begin to flourish. Be sure to journal about this topic and mark your next date of service on your calendar. Also, we want to see you in action! Snap a photo of you and your man serving and post it on Instagram or Facebook with the hashtag #14daychallenge for a potential repost.

Journal below:

Write what you learned today, how it went and what memories were made.

CHAPTER SEVEN
—
Pause for Celebration

In High School, I was a cheerleader, and every year we would volunteer by teaming up with our local 15K marathon events. We would set up a booth with water at the 5K mark, and we would cheer on all participants. Why were we cheering for them? They hadn't even crossed the finish line yet. However, we understood that celebrating their progress with them would encourage them to make it to the finish line.

Could the reason why many couples don't make it to the finish line of their dreams be because they fail to pause for celebration? To pause for celebration means you are not afraid to celebrate your progress and small victories. You may not be where you want to be in life yet, but with every passing day, you are one step closer. You have every reason to celebrate your small wins and progress! Don't wait until you make it to the finish line to celebrate with your partner. You may only be at the 5K mark of your dreams but pause for celebration because you are no longer at the starting line. The two of you are on your way to the finish line.

"This is the day that the Lord has made; let us rejoice and be glad in it." Psalm 118:24 (ESV)

Every waking day is a day the Lord has created for you and your partner to rejoice and be glad in. This Scripture doesn't teach us only to rejoice and be glad once we have conquered all our goals and dreams. It says this is the day to rejoice and be glad. Are you and your partner pausing for celebration in your life?

"Do not despise these small beginnings, for the Lord rejoices to see the work begin..." Zechariah 4:10 (NLT)

God is rejoicing over your small beginnings with your partner. He is excited to see the two of you work together to conquer what He has set before you. Who are we to despise the very thing that the Lord rejoices over?

Today, my husband and I challenge you and your partner to rejoice and pause for celebration. We would like for the two of you to create a list of the progress you have made together. Once you have completed this list, we want you to celebrate this progress by thanking God for how far you have come. We want you to encourage one another. Tell your partner how proud of him you are. Remind him that you are fighting together and his dreams matter to you. Remind him that he is not alone, and as a team, the two of you will conquer your goals. Lastly, we want you to praise God for what He has already done. Thank Him because He knows the end from the beginning. You may only be at the beginning, but God already has an ending in mind. So, thank Him because as you *"...delight in Him, He will give you the desires of your heart,"* per Psalm 37:4 (NIV). Jot down your experience and remember the best is yet to come.

Journal below:

Write what you learned today, how it went and what memories were made.

CHAPTER EIGHT

—

Disconnect from What's Disconnecting You

Distractions are everywhere, and they are Satan's tactic to steal, kill and destroy. Unfortunately, Satan is the god of the world we live in (2 Corinthians 4:4), which is why we need to be extremely careful to make sure he does not become the god of our relationships and marriages. Satan is not creative. He uses the same tactics today that he used many years ago. As we read the Bible, we learn that Satan distracted Martha with busyness. She was so busy serving she didn't have time to listen to Jesus's teaching and then got upset that her sister Mary wasn't distracted and was doing what was important, listening to the teaching of Jesus. Martha was unable to discern what was truly important, and I see this often happen today. Many couples are struggling due to distractions and because of the inability to discern what is truly important. Satan is killing marriages, but as women of God, we have power against the enemy and what God has brought together no one shall separate.

I ask that you take a moment to think about what distractions might be disconnecting you from your relationship. Is it busyness? Is it your cell phone? Could it be worry? Distractions come in many different shapes and sizes, but it is up to us to recognize what these distractions are so we can disconnect from what is disconnecting us. In my marriage, I've recognized that ministry and social media are two of my biggest distractions. There have been times when I have become so caught up in ministering to women that I failed to minister to my husband. There also have been times when I was so committed to posting a blog or a photo on Instagram that I was inattentive to my husband's needs. I realized being connected to this trend in my life causes me to be disconnected from my husband.

1 Timothy 3:5 (NIV) says, *"If anyone does not know how to manage his own family, how can he take care of God's church?"* Ladies, we must manage our marriage before anything else. Our relationships matter. If we don't learn to manage the distractions in our relationships, our distractions will manage our relationships. I refuse to allow distractions to disconnect me from my marriage. I have learned to put away all distractions. Every night at dinner time, I place my cell phone on *"Do not disturb."* I don't take ministry related calls past 6 P.M. unless it is a dire emergency. From time to time I will also go on a social media fast. I will quit using social media for a specific time. When I do this, not only do I spend more time with God, but I also spend more time with my husband. When I put away distractions

and stay focused, I tend to see the two most important relationships in my life grow! Doesn't that make you wonder why distractions are so tempting? Because if putting distractions away will better your relationship with God and with your partner, then Satan needs those distractions to pull you away from both. Don't let the devil win by pulling you away from God because if he can pull you away from God, then eventually he will pull you away from your partner.

Today, to keep your relationship fresh and on fire, my husband and I challenge you to disconnect from what's disconnecting you. We challenge you to fast all forms of social media for one day. Instead of going on social media, we want you to pray and send your partner an encouraging text throughout the day every time you are tempted with a distraction. If the two of you will be in each other's presence today, make sure to spend quality time together without the use of your cell phone. Write about your experience and remember - if you want your relationship to be prosperous and effective, don't forget to disconnect from whatever may be disconnecting you from your significant other.

Journal below:

Write what you learned today, how it went and what memories were made.

CHAPTER NINE
—
Consumed by Comparison

Have you ever compared your life to another's and thought that if you had what they had or looked the way they look, then your life would somehow be greater? I have. For many years I could not seem to find contentment with what I had or with who I was. In fact, I desperately tried to imitate other women in my life thinking it would make me more lovable. What I failed to realize is that comparing myself to others made me confused because I wasn't true to myself and I was not who God created me to be.

In the Bible, Paul shares one of my favorite Scriptures, *"Not that I was ever in need, for I have learned how to be content with whatever I have. I know how to live on almost nothing or with everything. I have learned the secret of living in every situation, whether it is with a full stomach or empty, with plenty or little. For I can do everything through Christ, who gives me strength."* Philippians 4:11-13 (NLT)

Paul was a free man because he could be content whether he had more or less than the people around him. He found that the secret to contentment is not found in how much money you have, how big your bra size is, or how small your waist is. Because the secret to contentment is not found in what you have, it is found in who you have, Jesus.

Friends, if we are not careful, we will begin to compare our lives and our relationships to those around us. The enemy would love to confuse God's plans for your life with His plans for another person's life. Just because your friends are getting married, having babies, or buying houses and you and your partner are struggling just to pay the bills does not mean you are behind in life. It does not mean that you're less valuable than them either. God's timing is always perfect, and He is doing work within you that you may not understand in this season of life.

When God allows us to struggle, He is not punishing us. He is preparing us, building our character, and building our foundation. God wants you to be so consumed with Him that like Paul you can be content in whatever season of life you are in. Whether you're dating or married, whether you're rich or poor, whether you're living out your dreams or taking steps to get there, you can still be content in Christ.

Be encouraged! God will finish the good work He has begun in your relationship. I want you to be committed to walking out God's call for your life and don't allow the thought of comparison to consume you one bit. Comparison will confuse you and discourage your partner. What you have in this season is exactly what you need. God is your provider, and He will always provide you with exactly what you need. My husband and I had to learn to live on God's daily bread for several years. That season was not easy, but we learned to trust God and His faithfulness.

Today, my husband and I encourage you to process with your partner. Are there any areas in your life that have been consumed by comparison? It could be in ministry, in your relationship/marriage, in your career, etc. We would like for you to write these things down and then destroy them. Rip this list up and throw it away. Then we want you two to declare aloud, *"I am content with who I am, with what I have, and with where I am in life. From this day forward I will find my contentment in Christ and will no longer be consumed by comparison."* Write about how doing this has improved your relationship. Remember that what God has for you will make its way to you. All you need to do is seek Him daily and allow Him to lead you and your relationship. A personal relationship with Christ will satisfy you and fulfill you more than anything else ever could.

Journal below:

Write what you learned today, how it went and what memories were made.

CHAPTER TEN
—
Love Keeps Record of Rights

"Love keeps no record of wrongs." 1 Corinthians 13:5

I used to be a living product of my mistakes. I know first-hand the danger of keeping a record of wrongs. I grew up in a household full of hurt and pain. When one would make a mistake, it was rarely forgotten. Our mistakes were continuously thrown into our faces. This was detrimental to my emotional health. I became afraid to make decisions because I was in fear that I would make the wrong one and get ridiculed for it.

I didn't learn until later in life that mistakes are a blessing from God. Through my mistakes, I learned more about myself and life than when I did something right.

In relationships, mistakes will be made, and accidents will happen; it's inevitable. It is how we process the mistakes with our partner that often becomes the make or break of the scenario. If you want to be in it for the long haul with your partner, you need to make him feel safe coming to you. He shouldn't feel like he is going to get ridiculed, or that you're going to *"forgive, but never forget."*

Remember, it's impossible to have a prosperous future with your partner if you choose to live in the past. Destroy all record of wrongs and begin to keep a record of rights! Love uplifts, love encourages, love brings safety, love brings hope, and love never gives up (see 1 Corinthians 13:4-8).

Today it is time to put to death all record of wrongs, and it is time to move forward into a blessed and prosperous future with your partner by collecting and keeping a record of rights. My husband and I challenge you and your partner to take 10-20 minutes (more if you need it) to write down a list of everything your partner has done right lately. We would like for the two of you to read your list to one another and hug it out. Thank your partner for everything he has done right. Be sure to journal about your experience, and from this point forward meditate on his rights and not on his wrongs.

Journal below:

Write what you learned today, how it went and what memories were made.

CHAPTER ELEVEN
—
The Little Things Matter

I learned at a very young age that the little things in life matter. Every Christmas my great grandma buys me a gift card. I excitedly open it in front of her, I thank her, and I give her a big hug. I will never forget how upset she became the time I failed to call her to tell her what I spent my gift card on. What my grandmother was trying to teach me is that the little things in life matter. The big hug I gave her at the moment meant nothing in comparison to the little follow-up phone call I could have given her after the fact. My grandmother wanted the opportunity to rejoice with me over the gift I purchased with the gift card she gave me. I never made that mistake again.

To some, this might seem like nonsense, and at the time I did not understand why she was so upset over such a little thing. As I grew up, I learned that in relationships the little things truly matter.

The Bible teaches us about the little things. We learn that with faith the size of a mustard seed, we can move mountains, if we are faithful in the little, we will be ruler over much, David slew a giant with a stone, and Jesus fed thousands with a fish given to Him by a little boy. Again, the little things matter because the little things have often made the greatest impacts.

When my husband and I were dating, I would pray every day and ask God to give me an encouraging and prophetic word for my future husband. I would then text my husband a word that would uplift his spirit and encourage him to continue fighting for God's promises. When my husband preaches, he most often mentions those text messages over any big thing I have done for him. Why? Because it's the little things that make the greatest impact in our hearts.

If David could slay a giant with a little stone, I wonder what giants we face in our relationships that could be slain by not overlooking the little things. If Jesus could miraculously feed thousands with a little fish, I wonder what miracles could happen in our marriages by not overlooking the little things. So today, don't overlook the power of a thank you. Don't overlook the power of a word of encouragement. Don't overlook the power of a lunch box note. These little seeds have a way of moving mountains in our relationships.

Today, my husband and I challenge you to make the little things in your relationship matter. In doing so, you will keep your love for him fresh and on fire. We believe that as you do this the level of honor will raise in your household. Feel free to use some of the examples provided above or come up with something on your own. Don't forget to journal your experience with day 11 of this challenge.

Journal below:

Write what you learned today, how it went and what memories were made.

CHAPTER TWELVE

—

Wisdom Seekers

The way I grew up sparked a desire within me to search for wisdom. My mother and father separated when I was 12 years old. They both worked hard, but we lived in a rented condo and never had an abundance of finances. There is nothing wrong with living this way. However, something inside of me always wanted more. Because of this, it is part of the reason I ended up in the adult film industry. Yes, I was looking for love and acceptance, but making more than $30,000 a month wasn't bad either. It was a poor decision, but this is why we need to seek wisdom.

I was 18 years old and thought I knew everything. I made poor decision after poor decision by myself, with no regard to what my elders had to say. I thought everyone around me was ignorant because I was *"walking in success."* But after many disappointments and much heartbreak, I realized that money doesn't equate to success. If your bank account is prosperous, but your soul is poor, then you have not found success at all. In fact, after seven years of selling myself for money, I left that industry with only $1,000 to my name. I was spending money faster than I was making it.

The day I met Jesus, He began to transform my way of thinking and gracefully taught me that I knew nothing. God did not create us to do life alone. The Holy Spirit began to show me people who were in my life that I needed to learn from. I began spending a lot of time with my grandma because she was 81 years old, had been married to my grandpa for more than 50 years, and had financial freedom. I also began to ask my uncle as many questions as my mind could come up with because he is a successful entrepreneur, has made millions of dollars, and has been married to my beautiful aunt for 20 years. What was I doing? I was getting advice. Why? Proverbs 19:20 (NIV) says, *"Listen to advice and accept discipline, and at the end, you will be counted among the wise."* I know that if I want to be successful in life, have a happy marriage that lasts a lifetime, and if I want to be counted as wise, then I need to seek wisdom at all cost. Proverbs 16:16 says that it is better to get wisdom and insight than silver and gold. Why? Because even a fool can get silver and gold, but wisdom will give you the ability to keep the silver and gold. In other words, even a fool can get married, but only wisdom will give a person the ability to stay married. Without wisdom, we are foolish, and without wisdom, we cannot sustain the blessings that God has for us. I love gaining wisdom from those who have been around longer than myself, because with it I can learn what to do and not to do, and have an even greater marriage because of it.

Today, my husband and I challenge you to become a wisdom seeker. What this looks like is that you will not try to do life on your own. We encourage to find a couple in your path that is living a life that inspires you and ask them out on a double date. Mentally prepare for this double date by thinking of some questions you need answers to. Make sure your questions are in alignment with the life they are living. If they have been married for 15 years, ask them the secret to their success. Whatever you need wisdom in, seek it from them. After your double date, make sure to journal the wisdom you gained. Remember, Proverbs 27:17 (NLT) says, *"As iron sharpens iron, so a friend sharpens a friend."* After your double date, you and your man are going to be sharper, wiser, and stronger.

Journal below:

Write what you learned today, how it went and what memories were made.

CHAPTER THIRTEEN

—

The Beauty in the Struggle

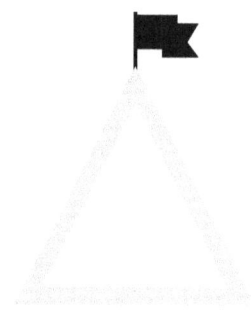

Until the age of 26, my life was a struggle. As a child, I struggled to find acceptance and as an adult searched heavily for it. My search landed me in the Adult Film industry for seven years. I found myself deep into depression, drug addiction, and often entertained suicidal thoughts. I was in a pit of darkness and saw no light at the end of the tunnel. I was hopeless until one day Jesus radically changed my life. He pulled me out of the pit and placed a mind-blowing call on my life. Since leaving the adult industry and stepping into my calling, I have globally preached the Gospel and have even appeared on ABC's *The View* with my friend, Craig Gross, founder of XXXchurch.com. Who would have thought that I would have gone from a porn star to a preacher? Certainly, not me, but that's the beauty of the struggle.

Much of my struggle as an adult was caused by my poor decision making. Many struggles can be avoided in life by seeking God, by seeking wise counsel, and by making good decisions. However, there is a struggle that we must all endure; one that cannot be avoided. The struggle is that no matter what you do, no matter how hard you pray, and no matter the amount of wise counsel you seek, you just can't seem to find a way out. This is a struggle that God allows because He wants to test and prepare you for the things He has in store for you. Every relationship will encounter this type of struggle; it is up to you and your partner to endure it and pray your way through it so that you can find the beauty in the struggle.

In Genesis 37, we are introduced to a man named Joseph. Joseph encountered many struggles but endured until the end. Because of his endurance and upright character, he found the beauty in the struggle. One night Joseph had a dream that he would become a king and that his family would bow down to him. When he shared this dream with his brothers, they hated him for it. Their hatred and jealousy towards their brother caused them to sell Joseph into slavery. Over the next several years, Joseph encountered some highs and plenty of lows. Joseph had to endure the unavoidable struggle, and because he did, his dream became a reality. After much struggle and more than a decade later, Joseph was made ruler over the land of Egypt. When there was a famine in the land, unbeknownst to Joseph's family, they bowed down to him and asked him for food for their family. Joseph's dream had finally become a reality.

Genesis 50:20 (NLT) sums up much of Joseph's struggles when he says to his family, *"You intended to harm me, but God intended it all for good. He brought me to this position so that I could save the lives of many."* Could it be that the reason your relationship encounters struggle is that your struggle is meant to bring you and your partner to a place where you could glorify God and save the lives of many? Joseph would have never become a ruler over Egypt had he not encountered constant struggle. I bet that you and your partner wouldn't get to where you're meant to be in life without the struggle. Where are your struggles leading you?

We must keep in mind that though we may struggle, God is still in control. Though people may have intended to harm you, God has intended it all for good. Did you notice the scripture said, *"God intended it all for good"?* Let this word encourage you today because God has intended, not some of your struggles, but all your struggles for good.

Today, my husband and I challenge you to talk about your struggles with your partner. Maybe the two of you are experiencing financial difficulties, or have recently experienced loss or disappointment. We believe that life is not a waiting room, but a classroom because while working toward your dreams, there are many lessons to be learned. We challenge you to make peace with your struggles by finding the beauty in the struggle. Here are a few questions to ask one another: What do you think God is trying to teach us through our present struggle? Do you think you have been allowing God to process you or have you been fighting it? Where do you think our present struggle is leading us? What lessons have you learned from our struggles? Journal your answers, so you have something to look back on when you're walking in the fullness of your dreams. Romans 8:28 (NLT) promises that *"God causes everything to work together for the good of those who love Him and are called according to His purpose for them."* With that promise in mind, do not worry, nor fear, because whatever battle you may be facing, God is working it together for your good.

Journal below:

Write what you learned today, how it went and what memories were made.

CHAPTER FOURTEEN
—
L.O.L Love Out Loud

This a spin on the classic L.O.L (Laugh Out Loud). Which is also important in every relationship, I mean, who wants to be in a relationship where there is no laughter? #Boring! However, we will be focusing in on Loving Out Loud.

Loving Out Loud is a term my husband and I use to express our gratitude toward one another. We have learned that an unexpressed compliment isn't a compliment at all. We make every effort to speak (out loud) all the good things on our minds about one another to each other.

Since the day I encountered Jesus, loving out loud has become a part of who I am. I never knew what it was like to be on the receiving end of Loving Out Loud. For a very large portion of my life, I was starving for affirmation. I didn't know what it was like hearing the words, *"I am proud of you."* I often felt rejected and rarely accepted by the words spoken to me by others. I do not believe we should live by the praise of others. However, I do believe our tongues are a powerful tool, and they have the power of life and death (Proverbs 18:21). Because I was never on the receiving end of loving out loud, I choose to go out of my way to give words of encouragement to the discouraged, and speak life to those I love, especially in my marriage. I have seen lives change and flourish because of this.

In a world that is well able to tell our men everything they aren't and everything they can't do, we need to be the type of women who encourage our men and speak life into them. Let's bring them confidence by giving them compliments and by speaking words of strength to them.

I love what the Bible teaches us in Proverbs 15:4 (MSG), *"Kind words heal and help; cutting words wound a maim."*

This Scripture teaches us that our kind words matter. They both heal and help. One kind word can help the position of your partner's heart. One kind word can bring him from a place of weakness into a place of strength.

Today, my husband and I challenge you to no longer be silent with your words, because love should never be silent. We challenge you to love out loud by refusing to hold back words of encouragement. Tell your partner the kind things you feel about him. You can do this through text, social media, or in person. If you choose to do this through social media, hashtag #14daychallenge for a potential repost. Have fun loving out loud, and make sure to journal about the experience.

Journal below:

Write what you learned today, how it went and what memories were made.

Thank you!

Thank you so much for joining us on this 14-day challenge. We love the fact that you care enough about your relationship to invest time into it. We hope that you learned more about one another, fell more in love, and grew closer to God during this 14-day challenge.

Each day you had a different challenge, but we encourage you to incorporate the challenges into your daily life so your relationship will continue to stay fresh and on fire.

We can't wait to hear all about your experiences! Hashtag #14daychallenge on social media. We will frequently check up on this hashtag to get to know you and your significant other. Again, thank you for joining us on this challenge.

Love Always,
Rich & Britt

BIO

Richard and Brittni De La Mora live in San Diego, CA. They are the directors of the young adult ministry called the Uprising at Cornerstone Church of San Diego and are the founders of Always Loved. They are evangelists, authors and make YouTube videos. You may have seen them on ABC's The View, CBN's The 700 Club, TBN Salsa, or National Geographic's Drugs Inc. They have a passion for bettering relationships, reaching the lost at all cost, and inspiring all people to live out their God-given potential.

Where to find us online

We love connecting with people on social media, so feel free to stop by and say hi, we would love to e-meet you!

INSTAGRAM

Rich: @Richardelamora

Britt: @Brittnidelamora

TWITTER

Britt: @Brittnidelamora

WEBSITES

Britt: Brittnidelamora.com

FACEBOOK

Rich: Richandbritt

Britt: Brittnidelamora

SNAPCHAT

Username: Brittnidelamora

www.ingramcontent.com/pod-product-compliance
Lightning Source LLC
Chambersburg PA
CBHW070208100426
42743CB00013B/3102